LAND TO INVESTORS:
Large-Scale Land Transfers in Ethiopia

Dessalegn Rahmato

FSS Policy Debates Series No.1

Forum for Social Studies (FSS)
Addis Ababa

Layouts: Konjit Belete

ISBN: 978-99944-50-40-4

Forum for Social Studies (FSS)
P.O. Box 25864 code 1000
Addis Ababa, Ethiopia
Email: fss@ethionet.et
Web: www.fssethiopia.org.et

This study was published with the financial support of the Royal Embassy of Denmark, Addis Ababa, Ethiopia.

Contents

Tables

Acronyms

BS:	Beni Shangul
EPA:	Environmental Protection Authority
EPDRF:	Ethiopian Peoples Democratic Revolutionary Front
EWCA:	Ethiopian Wildlife Conservation Agency
FAO:	Food and Agriculture Organisation
FDRE:	Federal Democratic Republic of Ethiopia
GTP:	Growth and Transformation Plan
HoAREC:	Horn of Africa Regional Environmental Conservation
IFPRI:	International Food Policy Research Institute
IIED:	International Institute for Environment and Development
IUCN:	International Union for the Conservation of Nature
MDGs:	Millennium Development Goals
MME:	Ministry of Mines and Energy
MOA:	Ministry of Agriculture
MOARD:	Ministry of Agriculture and Rural Development
MOFED:	Ministry of Finance and Economic Development
NBC:	National Biofuel Corporation (Ethiopia)
OCHA:	Office for the Coordiantion of Humanitarian Affairs (UN)
Oro:	Oromia
PASDEP:	Plan for Accelerated and Sustained Development to End Poverty
PSNP:	Productive Safety Net Program
REDD:	Reducing Emissions from Deforestation and Degradation
Rs:	Rupees (Indian)
SNNP:	Southern Nations, Peoples and Nationalities
TFCI:	Trans-Frontier Conservation Initiative Task Force
USD:	United States Dollar

Acknowledgement

Financial assistance for this study was provided by LANDac, the IS Academy on Land Governance for Equitable and Sustainable Development, in the Netherlands. LANDac is a partnership of International Development Studies, Utrecht University, African Studies Centre, Agriterra, Disaster Studies - Wageningen University, Hivos, Royal Tropical Institute (KIT), Triodos-Facet and the Netherlands Ministry of Foreign Affairs. Website: www.landgovernance.org

About the author

DESSALEGN RAHMATO, a Senior Research Fellow at FSS, is a specialist in agrarian studies but has also undertaken research work on other rural subjects. He has published numerous works on land rights, food security and rural poverty. His most recent book, entitled *The Peasant and the State: Studies in Agrarian Change in Ethiopia* was published in 2008. He is the winner of the 1999 Prince Claus Award given by the Prince Claus Fund of the Netherlands in recognition of significant achievements in the field of research and development.

Abstract

LAND TO INVESTORS: Large-Scale Land Transfers in Ethiopia

Under its program of land investments, the Ethiopian government has leased out huge tracts of land to domestic and foreign investors on terms that are highly favorable to both but particularly to foreign ones. Critical reports on the "bonanza" reaped by foreign capital have appeared in the world media and the websites of international activist organizations, and while some of these are based on questionable evidence, the global attention they have drawn may well be deserved given the image of the country as a land of poverty and hunger. The lands transferred are said to be "unused" public lands but include arable, pasture, woodland and forest, wetlands, water sources and wildlife habitats, and farmers, pastoralists and minority groups and their communities affected by the investment program have contested the investments. The government's stated objectives are that large-scale investments will benefit the country from increased foreign earnings, will create employment opportunities, enable the transfer of technology to small-holders, and provide infrastructure and basic services to local communities but what is happening at the moment suggests that many of these objectives will not be met. This study, which is based on information gathered from field interviews as well as other sources, looks at the subject from a land rights perspective, with emphasis on the relations of power between small land-users and their communities on the one hand and the state on the other. At bottom what is at stake is the land and the resources on it, and what is being "grabbed" are rights that in most cases belong to peasant farmers, pastoralists and their communities. In the long run, the shift of agrarian system from small-scale to large-scale, foreign-dominated production -which is what the investment program is now doing- will marginalize small producers, and cause immense damage to local ecosystems, wildlife habitats and biodiversity.

1. Introduction

The catch-phrase, "global land grab", refers to the rush for commercial land in Africa and elsewhere by private and sovereign investors for the purpose of growing food and bio-fuel crops for the export market, and, in which, the land deals concluded have gone largely to benefit foreign capital. The phenomenon has attracted the attention of the world media, international activist organizations, donor groups and others since much of the land given out is in poor and vulnerable countries that have long been dependent on food aid and other support programs provided by Western donor agencies. Global land grabbing has spread quite rapidly following the international food crisis of the second half of the 2000s which saw exceptionally high commodity prices and severe supply shortages in the world market. The crisis aggravated vulnerabilities in many poor countries, but also raised the specter of food insecurity among those which hitherto had relied on the global food market. It placed the quest for national food security as an important policy agenda not only in poor nations but also in countries which were capital-rich but had limited agricultural endowments, as well as those which were faced with high populations, a burgeoning middle class and high demand for food stuffs. According to international media reports, market analysts are of the opinion that volatility in the world food trade will continue to drive up commodity prices and to cause periodic global shortages for many years to come. There is thus a strong food security element in the global land grab, though one should also note that for investors from the Gulf countries and Asia, which are playing the lead role at present, the opportunity for profits provided in many African countries has also been an important driving force. African countries have offered a favorable investment climate, seemingly abundant land, low land rents and labor costs, and few restrictions on production and export. As of the end of 2009, more than a dozen countries in Africa, including Ethiopia, had given out millions of hectares of farm land to foreign capital under highly concessionary terms (see Cotula *et al* 2009, IFPRI 2009, World Bank 2010).

In the case of Ethiopia, what has attracted worldwide interest is the extent of the land given out to foreign investors within a short space of time and the conditions under which this was done. As we shall see later in this study, investors from the Middle East and Asia have received land measuring from 50 to 100 thousand hectares at rental fees of two to five U.S dollars per hectare per year[1]. Critical reports about the "bonanza" reaped by foreign capital have appeared in the world media and the websites of international activist

---

[1] Since the draft of this paper was completed MOA(RD) has issued new reports and figures on land investments. See "Notes on Information Update" in Annex 1.

organizations[2], and while some of them are based on questionable evidence, the global attention they have drawn may well be deserved given the image of the country as a land of poverty and hunger.

Ethiopia is one of the poorest countries in the world, and since the decades of the 1960s has suffered severe food shortages and famines on numerous occasions. As recently as 2002/03, there was widespread starvation in many parts of the country affecting more than 13 million rural people, and it required large inflows of international food aid to avert a tragedy on the scale of the famine of 1985/86 when hundreds of thousands of peasants and pastoralists perished in the worst tragedy in the country's history. Malnutrition is endemic in the countryside as well as in the urban areas, and diseases associated with poor nutrition and scarcity of clean water are common. In 2009, over 22 percent of the rural population was dependent on a combination of emergency food aid and safety net programs financed by Western countries and international agencies. While the number of people seeking emergency food assistance has decreased since then, nearly eight million rural people continue to be supported by safety net programs[3]. On the other hand, there has been a fairly high rate of economic growth in the last ten years and improvements in health services have been registered, nevertheless this has not made a significant impact on rural poverty nor has it helped to ensure food security to a great number of farming households.

---

[2] See References for international media coverage; activist websites include www.grain.org; www.oaklandinstitute.org ; www.foeeurope.org
[3] Regular updates of the country's food security situation is available on OCHA's website: http://ochaonline.un.org/Ethiopia . See also Dessalegn 2010a.

2.   The Approach of the Study

The debate on the global land rush has been dominated by those who have focused on what they believe to be the exploitive nature of land investments and the loss of essential resources by rural populations, especially in Africa where such investments are taking place on a large scale and where most governments are actively encouraging it. This is the approach taken by international activist organizations which have argued that the acquisition of land by foreign entities in poor and vulnerable countries poses a threat to the livelihoods of the people and endangers their chances of achieving food security and improved nutrition. The more polemical version of this line of argument speaks of a new form of agricultural neo-colonialism, and accuses the international financial institutions of promoting aggressive land grabs through support to investors and host governments[4]. A second approach, favored by liberal and pragmatic opinion, sees immense dangers in the global rush for land but recognizes that there are considerable opportunities that could benefit host governments and their populations. The optimists here believe that given responsible decision-making and equally responsible investment, the costs and damages assumed to be inherent in land grabbing could be minimized, leading to a situation where both host countries and investors could benefit in equal measure. Proponents focus on the need for better land administration, improved quality and transparency of land deals and greater institutional capacity of host countries for contract management, oversight and follow-up. Emphasis is placed on the importance of establishing sound guidelines and standards for land allocations and land use, and an effective code of conduct to govern relations between investors on the one hand, and communities and host governments on the other. This is basically the standpoint of international agencies such as FAO and the World Bank and also of works produced under the aegis of international research bodies such as IFPRI, IIED and others[5].

A third line of argument looks at the structural changes that large-scale land transfers will bring about in host countries, especially in the agricultural sector and the direction these changes will take in terms of class divisions and social polarization. Borras and Franco (2010) are critical of the liberal approach and contend that the debate should examine what they call the political dynamics of land property relations and changes in these relations, and give particular attention to class analysis. The impact of the global land grab, they argue, is to bring about changes in land property relations favoring the (re)concentration of

---

[4] See articles by the Oakland Institute and GRAIN: www.oaklandinstitute.org , www.grain.org
Short pieces on agricultural neo-colonialism have appeared on GRAIN web pages. A recent
international conference on land grabbing held in the Netherlands was titled "Africa for Sale".
[5] FAO 2010; World Bank 2009, 2010; IFPR 2009; Cortula et al (IIED) 2009; see also Schoneveld
et al 2010

wealth and power in the hands of the dominant classes, especially landed groups, capitalists, corporate entities, state bureaucrats and village chiefs. Such changes are happening and have given rise to the dispossession and displacement of smallholders, indigenous peoples and the poor in general. Building on this line of thought, Ruth Hall (2010) shows that the common trend of the changes in question is towards what she calls the "South Africanisation" of agrarian structures, meaning structures dominated by large, settler-type estates existing side by side with a host of impoverished small farms struggling to survive in the shadow of these estates.

My purpose in this study is not to present a critique of the general literature nor point out what I consider to be deficiencies in some of the studies noted above, though I should point out in passing that I share some of the criticism of the liberal (and "code of conduct") approach presented in Borras and Franco. My aim here is to draw attention to what I believe to be a gap in the debate, which is that sufficient attention has not been given to the issue of land rights of communities and the state-power dynamics that are intertwined with such rights in host countries. In some cases, the urge for greater state power centralization appears to have been the driving force for the commercialization of land and the open door policy governments have extended to investment capital, both domestic and foreign. From this perspective the global land grab will have had the effect of enhancing the dominance of the state at the expense of citizens and grassroots communities. Stated briefly, the point is this: at bottom what is at stake is the land and the resources on it, and what is being grabbed or transferred are rights belonging to individuals and communities despite the claims of governments that the lands in question are "unused" public lands and do not belong to anyone.

Attempts at examining large-scale land transfers and their economic, social and environmental impact in Ethiopia have been quite limited, though this will soon change as interest on the subject among social scientists, the media, independent organizations and the public is now growing. In the last three to four years environmental activist groups have prepared for public discussion a number of critical reports on the heightened interest expressed by foreign investors on growing bio-fuel crops and the lands that have been offered to them for this purpose[6]. These reports have focused primarily on bio-fuel production and its environmental consequences but have largely ignored the equally large land transfers for the raising of food and agro-industry crops, ranching and meat

---

[6] See Ensermu et al 2009; Green Forum 2010; Hecket and Negusu 2008; and Melca Mahiber 2008 for these reports. Recently, Imeru Tamrat (2010) has prepared a paper on the legal and institutional framework of large-scale investments in Ethiopia for the World Bank

processing, and the impact both measures have had on land rights, food security and access to resources.

The commercialization of land and the shift to large scale agriculture is being presented by the Ethiopia government and international bodies such as the World Bank as an essential measure for agricultural modernization and the improvement of productive efficiency which is said to lead to increased food production and economic growth (MOARD 2008, 2010; World Bank 2010). The World Bank argues that increased demand for food products in the developing world will be driven by population growth, expanding urbanization, and rising incomes and this demand will have to be met by bringing more land into cultivation and by improving productivity. The Bank expects Africa to benefit immensely because, it says, potential farmland is plentiful and and productivity on land currently under cultivation is very low compared to what could be achieved. The Ethiopian government, as we shall later in this paper, also believes that the country has plenty of "unused" land which can be operated efficiently by large-scale investors without posing a threat to the livelihood of smallholders. Moreover, an additional rational that is driving its open-door policy is the need to boost export crops and earn increased foreign currency. We shall see in the course of this discussion that the "land is plentiful" argument is, in large measure, untenable and that severe contradictions have arisen in the actual process of land transfers. The reality on the ground is that in many cases the rights of smallholders, who have been utilizing the lands in question for many generations, are being compromised and in some cases sacrificed for what public officials regard as the greater national good.

Putting the rights of smallholders at the center of the discussion enables us to bring in the state and the question of governance since embedded in the concept of land rights are relations of power between the state on the one hand and individuals and communities on the other. The land transfers that have taken place on an unprecedented scale in the last ten to twelve years has brought to the surface several issues of public concern. First, it is the first time in this country that so much land - perhaps as much as a million hectares at present and expected to increase substantially in the coming years- has been put *in the hands of foreign investors*. Total transfers from the late 1990s to the end of 2008 to both domestic and foreign capital reaches almost 3.5 million hectares according to the database compiled by MOARD (2009a). The significance of this is that the state is now redefining the agrarian structure of the country as well as the future course of agricultural production in a manner that will increasingly marginalize the rural population. Secondly, since, by law, the state has juridical ownership of the land and in contrast peasant farmers and pastoralists have the right of use only, it is the state which in effect has been responsible for land grabbing: it has used its statutory right of ownership to alienate land from those who have customary rights and rights of longstanding usage, and transferring it, without consultation or consent, to investors from outside the communities concerned as well as from outside the country itself. The commercialization of land has served as a political advantage to the state since it enhances its power vis-à-vis rural communities, and leads to the greater concentration of authority in the hands of public agents and local administrators. The presence of large farms in rural communities operating with modern technologies will be a constant reminder of the danger hanging over small farmers and pastoralists and their way of life.

Moreover, as we shall see in more detail in the pages that follow, the land investment program is flawed and full of risks for the following reasons: a) land was given away to investors by the government without consulting the local communities concerned and taking their rights and interests into account; b) when the program is fully implemented by 2015, as the government has planned, there will be a concentration of land in the hands of a few which will give rise to class antagonisms in the countryside; and c) the program does not address the food security concerns of the country.

This study is based on a wide variety of source material, the most important of which include findings from field work in several communities affected by investor projects in Gambella and Oromia *Killils*[7], interviews with public officials at federal, Killil and *woreda* levels, interviews with smallholders and others in the communities concerned, and documents and data from federal and Killil public agencies. I have also made use of secondary sources, both published and unpublished, material from web sources, and articles from both the international and local media. More details about the methodology, sources and some of the difficulties we faced in gathering information are given in Annex 2 at the end.

---

[7] In this work I have employed the term "*Killil*" in preference to "Region".

3.   State and Land

It will take too far to examine the state and the land system and the legal and policy instruments that have shaped the latter in the last decade and half, but a brief review of the tenure regime now in place will have to suffice for the purposes of this discussion. Without an understanding of the land system it will be difficult to explain how large tracts of land were transferred to foreign and domestic investors in a short space of time without the knowledge and consent of land users and rural communities on the ground.

The federal and Killil constitutions as well as land laws issued so far declare that all land in the country –urban and rural- is state property and private ownership is not allowed[8]. Land users (cultivators and pastoralists) have only use rights over the land in their care which they cannot sell, mortgage or exchange in any way. The power to administer land, which includes land allocation, registration and adjudication, has been given by law to the Killil authorities but such administration must be consistent with the federal constitution issued in 1995 and federal land laws, the most recent of which were issued in 2005. The use right of land holders is dependent on residence in a *kebelle*, personal engagement in farm activities, "proper" management of the land, and other restrictive conditions which we need not discuss here. Holders who are found to have violated any of these conditions are subject to penalties including the loss of their right to the land. In some Killils, holders may also lose the land if they are absent from their farms and the land is left idle for three or more consecutive years. The government has the right to remove holders from the land if it decides that the land is needed for "public purposes" or if it considers that the land will be more valuable if utilized by investors, cooperative societies and other public or private entities. The government will pay compensation in the event of land expropriation but many holders whose land has been alienated have often complained that the compensation paid has been unfair and inadequate.

The government has implemented a program of land certification and registration in the last ten years, and while the program has been welcomed by many land holders, it has not prevented public authorities from expropriating land and natural resources. In this same period a considerable number of peasants have been expropriated and their land leased out to private investors, especially from the early 2000s when land for the floriculture business, which was booming at the time, was in high demand. In brief, what we have is a land system, based essentially on state ownership, in which holders have rights that are conditional and subject to abrogation at any time, and in which they do not enjoy robust security of tenure. In the past as well as today, land rights have

---

[8] I have discussed the land system and relevant legislations at length in Dessalegn 2009.

always defined relations of power between the state on the one hand, and smallholders and their communities on the other (though the specific circumstances of and justifications for these relations have been different under different political contexts), and, in all cases, the defining element of these relations has been "conditional" or "dependent" land rights. Land dependency creates insecurity, "dis-empowers" individuals and communities, and enhances the hegemonic authority of the state. Here the state assumes the role of sole active agent, and individuals and communities become passive recipients of decisions from above because of the underlying insecurity over their property and the fear of losing it at any time. This is what "state" ownership of land has done in this country: as will be shown later in this paper, government authorities can give away land to investors and others without consulting land holders or their communities, and irrespective of the damage this may have on peasants' livelihoods and the natural environment.

In contrast, we may speak of "sovereign" land rights or "land sovereignty" which is grounded in *secure* rights of holders that enable them effective control and use of the *land as well as the natural resources in their community*; such resources are essential for the livelihood of individuals and households. We cannot separate individuals from their communities because one is not viable without the other; similarly the individual farm is insufficient to cover all the family's needs without access to the common resources that by customary right belong to the community. Such resources include pasture and grassland, woodland or forest land, water sources, sources of useful plants, transit corridors and pathways. Government land cover inventory, which depends on data obtained by satellite imagery, puts the extent of the "cultivated area" of the country (meaning land under cultivation by peasants, agro-pastoralists and others) as being less than 20 percent of the total land area, and it is argued on this basis that there is plenty of unused land to be handed out to investors. However, this is misleading because the term "cultivated area" is a narrow designation and does not include land from which peasants and agro-pastoralists access resources vital for their livelihood (see WBISPP 2004). Land sovereignty *empowers* holders and their communities, allowing them to be *active* agents in all matters affecting their lives.

From an another standpoint, the dominant power of the state has also been justified as necessary under the current state ideology on grounds of what its advocates call its developmental mission. The rationale for declaring the state the legitimate and sole actor in society was clearly spelt out in a document issued for leaders and cadres of the ruling Party in 2007. The document draws a distinction between what it calls "developmental" actors and rent-seeking or "rentier" ones. The latter are said to be guided by selfish motives, and seek personal gains in the form of wealth, property and status, while the former are dedicated to the development of the country and the progress of the people. In Ethiopia today, it is argued, all civil society organizations, opposition political parties, individuals and groups in private enterprise, and other groups are described as rent-seeking entities, while in contrast EPRDF, the ruling Party, is claimed to be the only one which has developmental credentials. Hence only the EPRDF has the ideological and moral legitimacy to hold power and only it is justified in serving as the sole active force in the country[9]. Moreover, economic development, which, it is argued, is best achieved under the guiding hands of the state, is another instrument used for legitimation of hegemonic power. Such state-led or "managed" development is invariably non-participatory since in the nature of things important policy decisions and program choices are made by central authorities which often are not accountable to anyone. This centralization has been made all the more powerful over the years because the country's Parliament continues to be a rubber-stamp institution, the dominant source of public information is the government-controlled media (the independent press has been stifled) and civil society institutions have lost what little voice they had.

The strategy of "managed" agricultural development and the subsequent turn towards large-scale production has thrown up a host of contradictions impacting on land allocation, administration, contract management and oversight. We shall discuss some of the important ones in the pages that follow but for now it may be useful to cite a few examples. The most obvious is the institutional instability that has become a regular part of the public sector. Since new initiatives are often decided upon by a small group at the top, there are frequently hasty changes to rules and regulations, established procedures of policy implementation are bypassed, stakeholder agencies are not consulted, and agencies least able to perform the tasks involved are given the most far-reaching responsibilities. As the mistakes and damages inevitable in such a process begin to pile up there are hasty attempts at crisis management and damage limitation.

---

[9] FDRE 2007. For more discussion of the arguments see Dessalegn 2010b.

4.   Large-Scale Land Deals

4.1   Open Door Policy

For nearly a decade from the mid-1990s, when the broad framework of the government's development strategy was formulated, agriculture, in particular crop cultivation, was given a commanding role and expected to serve as the engine of growth for the national economy as a whole. The strategy was not only rural-centered but stood on the shoulders of peasant farmers who were expected to provide not only the stimulus for development but also the surplus for food self-sufficiency. To this end, increased support was provided to smallholders both through domestic resources as well as through donor assistance, in the form of new technology packages, improved farming and resource management practices, credit services, and a variety of human capacity development programs. Government policy was decidedly biased in favor of smallholders and the land system put in place was considered to be peasant friendly[10]. This strategic focus began to shift slowly and subtly from the early years of the 2000s. The first indication of this impending shift maybe found in a document published in 2001 by the government setting out its rural development policy and strategies. While emphasis was still placed on the critical role of small farmers, the document establishes an important role for large-scale agricultural enterprises and foreign investors. The document speaks of an inevitable "role change" from peasant cultivation to capitalist farming, from small entrepreneur to large foreign investor. The following quote provides the arguments for the anticipated change:

> Private investors are already making a significant contribution to agricultural development. .. Experiences of developed economies clearly show that as an economy grows there is a tendency for some small farmers to quit the sector and seek employment in other sectors, and there are others who accumulate enough capital to go big in the sector. This implies that there is a direct correlation between agricultural growth and the role of private investment in the sector. This in turn means that assuming the objective of accelerated agricultural development is achieved, it is likely that there will be a role change. The key actor in the sector's development will be relatively large-scale private investors and not the semi subsistence small farmers.

> There are two investment areas that seem to be particularly suited for foreign investment in the agricultural sector. The first is to develop here-to-for unutilized vast land with high irrigation possibility. ... The second investment opportunity is to produce high-value agricultural products (e.g. flowers, vegetables) where the scale of operation could be small or medium ... ...   The country's demand for

---

[10] For an extended discussion of government agricultural policy in this period see the essays in Taye (ed) 2008.

participation in both areas is immense, and assurances are given that government institutions at all levels will do their level best to facilitate and assist foreign investors.

While …. underlying the importance of encouraging domestic private investment through well-conceived incentives, the focus of attention should be on attracting foreign investors. Historically, efforts made to attract foreign investment are almost exclusively directed towards non-agricultural sectors. This needs to change if Ethiopia is to achieve its agricultural objectives[11].

Other public documents also allude to the emerging "role change" in a variety of ways. The government's last poverty reduction document, PASDEP, the drafting of which began in 2004, states that one of the eight pillars of the government's development strategy is what it calls "a massive push" for accelerated growth, which is grounded on two policy thrusts, namely, the commercialization of agriculture and acceleration of private sector development (MOFED 2006). But the most significant initiative that was to serve as the basis for attracting foreign investment and encouraging large-scale agriculture were the legislative instruments put in place in 2002 and 2003, of which the investment proclamations and the regulations governing incentives provided to foreign and domestic investors are particularly noteworthy.

The investment legislation is very generous to foreign investors. The capital requirements of foreign businesses wishing to invest in the country ranges from zero (for those which export 75 percent or more of their output), to 25,000 USD (if they are in joint venture with domestic investors), to 100,000 USD. Foreign investors have the right to fully repatriate, in convertible currency, profits and dividends, principal and interest payments on external loans, proceeds from technology transfers as well as asset sales in the event of liquidation of the investment, and proceeds from the transfer of shares or ownership to a domestic investor. Expatriates employed in an enterprise may remit in foreign currency salaries and other payments accruing from their employment. Investors, foreign or domestic, are guaranteed against expropriation or nationalization except as required by the public interest. In the event this happens full compensation will be paid at the prevailing market value and foreign investors may repatriate this in hard currency (FDRE 2002a, 2003a).

Subsequent regulations issued by the Council of Ministers (FDRE 2003b, 2008b) provide attractive financial incentives. Any investment project, foreign or domestic, engaged in agriculture and other sectors which exports more than 50 percent of its output is eligible for income tax exemption for five years or more, while projects which export less than this are entitled to only two years'

---

[11] MOFED 2003.The document appeared in Amharic in 2001, and was translated into English in 2003.

exemption. Investors are also allowed to import, free of custom duty, all capital goods, construction materials and spare parts for the establishment or upgrading of their enterprise. In brief (and this is an important point for our discussion) strong encouragement is given to investors that *export* their products: investment projects planning to export more of their products are given greater benefits than those which do not. The shift towards large-scale agriculture is thus driven by the priority for exports and foreign earnings and *ignores the need for domestic food security.*

From 2007 onwards the federal and Killil governments were actively promoting land investments and seeking foreign capital. For this purpose a number of promotional documents were prepared, some of which were posted on the website of the Ministry of Agriculture and Rural Development (MOARD). Both Killil agencies and MOARD were keen to inform prospective investors that the country possessed "abundant land" suitable for a wide variety of crops and sufficient water resources, and that land transfers to investors would be made under favorable conditions. These resources were claimed to be unused by peasants, herders or others and their utilization by investors would not pose any threat to the livelihood of the populations concerned. MOARD has issued conflicting figures on how much land is available for investment. A document posted on its website in 2008 pointed out that the country's total land area measures 111.5 million hectares of which more than 74 million is said to be "suitable for annual and perennial crop production". Only 18 million hectares, the document notes, is currently under cultivation, thus suggesting that some 54 million is available for investment projects. The document further states that there is a "strong commitment from the government to make these fertile lands" available to investors who have the "capital and technology" to utilize them. However, the same document provides a considerably reduced estimate in later pages: the land said to be available in each of the Killils is estimated to be about 10 million hectares   -still enormous by any standards (MOARD 2008)[12]. However, senior officials of MOARD have given much reduced figures in press interviews and public statements in 2009 and 2010; they have reduced the estimate to between 3 to 3.5 million hectares. In an interview I had with an expert at MOARD in the second half of 2010, the figure given to me was 5 million hectares.

On the other hand, the Ministry of Mines and Energy's (MME) bio-fuel strategy document argues that the country possesses 24 million hectares of unutilized land suitable for growing bio-ethanol and bio-diesel crops, and leasing out these lands will not interfere with the production of food crops and not jeopardize the

---

[12] This and other documents, posted in www.moard.gov.et in 2009 and mid-2010, have since been removed.

country's plans for food security. The document notes that the government is determined to promote energy security by increasing the utilization of bio-fuels from local sources and reducing its dependence on imported fossil fuels. Bio-energy production will be undertaken by foreign and local investors with the government providing the land, financial incentives and other support (MME 2007). Overall, the wide discrepancy in the figures given by public agencies indicates that in many cases the authorities have not carried out an accurate and credible land suitability assessment, and that there is a good measure of guess work and arbitrariness in land estimations.

In 2008, the government decided to designate a lead agency for large-scale land deals with foreign and local investors, and the federal MOARD was chosen for this purpose. Its responsibility included preparing information and other technical inputs to attract investors, signing contracts with and transferring lands to those eligible, and undertaking follow-up and oversight. MOARD was to receive and administer all consolidated investment lands measuring 5000 hectares or more from the Killils. These lands were to be put into what was called a federal land bank to be accessed by investors through MOARD[13]. While all aspects of the land deals were to be concluded by and through MOARD, the income from the transactions, namely land rent, income tax, and other payments were to be utilized for the benefit of the Killils concerned. This change of procedure and division of responsibility was formally endorsed by a directive issued by the Council of Ministers in early 2010 (FDRE 2010). The Killils will continue to allocate land to investors as they had done prior to this decision but the lands in question will be ones measuring less than 5000 hectares and not part of the land they had submitted to the federal land bank. Some Killils were said to possess enormous land potential, and the transfer of some of it to the federal land bank was not seen as depriving them of the power of making land deals with investors. Thus Beni-Shangul is estimated to have as much as 1.4 million hectares potentially available for investors, Gambella 1.2 million, and SNNP 500,000, Oromia1.7 million (MOARD 2008; 2009c)

The earlier procedure for finalizing land deals was the responsibility of the Killil Investment Commissions, after the environmental soundness of the investment projects was approved by the the Killil counterpart of the federal EPA. EPA was given, by law, the authority to review and approve environmental impact assessment reports, which, as a rule, were prepared by the projects themselves (FDRE 2002b,c). The law on the matter was clear: no project was to be undertaken without approval given by EPA, and EPA or its subunits in the Killils were mandated to undertake follow-up and supervision to ensure that projects undertook their contractual obligations with regard to environmental

---

[13] Within MOARD, the unit responsible is the Agricultural Investment Support Directorate

considerations. This responsibility of EPA was transferred to MOARD in 2009 by means of an exchange of letters and a memorandum of understanding between the two agencies, even though MOARD did not have the technical and institutional capacity to carry out the duties involved.

Since 2009, a number of Killils have "voluntarily" transferred land to the federal land bank as shown in the Table below. There is anecdotal evidence (which we were unable to confirm) that some Killils were reluctant to transfer land, and that they may have done so under pressure.

Table 1. Investment Land under Federal Land Bank* 2010

Killils	Land in Hectares
Amhara	420,000 (not yet transfered)
Afar	409,678
BeniShangul	691,984
Gambella	829,199
Oromia	1,057,866
SNNP	180,625
Total	**3,589,678**

SOURCE: MOARD 2009c, 2010a; interviews with Oromia land and environment bureau
*NOTE: The figures given here have now changed. See Table A1, Annex 1 at the end

The new five-year Growth and Transformation Plan (GTP), which is to run from 2011 to 2015, and which was launched in the last quarter of 2010, envisages agriculture to grow at the rate of 14.9 % annually, and expects to double farm output by the year 2015. The Plan predicts that the country will meet all the MDG targets in 2015, and by 2028 Ethiopia will become what it calls a "middle income" country. One of the strategies for rapid agricultural growth is to be private investment in large-scale farms for which the government will provide support and encouragement. The land expected to be transferred to large-scale investors in the Plan period (not including land already allotted) is expected to increase from 0.5 million hectares in 2011, to 2.8 million in 2013 and 3.3 million in 2015 (see MOFED 2010 a,c).

4.2   Land to Investors

The allocation of farm land to investors in various parts of the country has been going on since the second half of the 1990s, but in the period up to the second half of 2002 those requesting land were predominantly local investors and the land granted was for the most part small in size, frequently less than 500 hectares. Foreign investors began to show keen interest following the enactment of the investment proclamation and as the success of the floriculture business in winning a growing market in Europe and elsewhere became apparent. The years between 2003 and 2007 were the boom years for cut flower exports in this country. The demand for land by investors, particularly foreign ones, began to increase sharply from 2006, and in 2008 there was what amounted to a mad rush to get access to land by both groups, with many applicants requesting large tracts, often measuring 10,000 hectares or more. More than one-third of the land allocated to investors by the Killils in the period up to 2008 was given out in that year.

Data obtained from MOARD shows that in the period between 1996 and the end of 2008, some 8000 applications for land were approved by the Killils with the total land committed measuring over three million hectares. The great majority of investors held the land idle (many simply did not have the resources to put the land to use) and some used it for purposes for which it was not approved. The record shows that slightly less than 20 percent of applicants had began project implementation and operation. Of the 8000 approved investment projects more than one-third are small enterprises holding 100 hectares or less and engaged in coffee hulling and washing, flower growing, animal fattening, dairy production, and fruit and vegetable growing. The figures given here must be taken with some caution because the data set from MOARD is not internally consistent. Data covering some eighteen years provided by the federal Investment Agency is virtually unhelpful because it is not sufficiently disaggregated.

In the period between 2003 and 2009 a considerable number of foreign investors were granted land either on their own or as part of joint ventures with local business, with total holdings measuring about one million hectares. The largest foreign holding is by Karuturi, a company based in Bangalore, India, which has been given 300,000 hectares of land in Gambella[14] and 11,000 in Bako Tibee woreda in Oromia. As a rule, the size of land allocated to foreign investors is much bigger than that of domestic investors: the justification given by public

---

[14] The record at the Investment Commission in Gambella shows only 100,000 hectares under Karuturi's name; I have been told by an official at MOARD that Karuturi's claim of 300,000 hectares has not been officially confirmed but all written sources I have consulted cite this figure. Since the draft of this paper was completed MOARD has announced that it has reduced the size of the company's holdings to 100,000 to protect wildlife in the area.

officials is that the foreign ones are much better endowed in terms of capital and technology and thus much better placed to make a success of their operations. On the other hand, in the last two years, that is 2009 and 2010, close to 500,000 hectares of land was allotted to investors both by MOARD and the Killils. The World Bank (2010) puts the total land transferred to investors in Ethiopia between 2004 and 2008 at 1.2 million hectares. The evidence available suggests that by the end of the GTP period in 2015, the total land transferred to investors will measure seven million hectares or more. A partial list of some of the larger land acquisitions is given in Table A2 in Annex 1. The list, which shows only a small percentage of the land deals so far concluded, includes only "large" transfers, that is land measuring 2000 hectares or more. In terms of absolute numbers, small-scale land transfers, i.e lands measuring below 500 hectares are much more numerous.

Investors' interests fall into two broad areas: there are those that are chiefly engaged in growing food or agro-industry crops, with the main food crops preferred being rice, maize, pulses and edible oil crops (sesame being an important one), while cotton and sugar cane are the agro-industry crops of choice. Other investors are using the land for biofuel production, and grow palm oil trees, *jatropha curcas*, and castor oil trees. This does not mean there is always a rigid division between one and the other; some may engage in both types of farming while a few others grow sugar cane only, which can be used for food as well as biofuel. On the other hand, a few privileged investors such as Sheikh Mohammed Al-Amoudi, a Saudi national with a strong link in Ethiopia and said to be one of the richest men in the Middle East, have multiple interests and varied investments. The Sheikh controls, through his numerous companies established in Ethiopia, extensive agricultural lands and plantations in various Killils. These lands include a large tea estate, over seven large-scale ranches for raising livestock and processing dairy and poultry products both for the home and export market, and extensive plantations for growing biofuel, food and industrial crops. His newly established mult-purpose firm, Horizon-Ethiopia Investments, has submitted a request for 100,000 hectares of land in Gambella to grow palm oil and other biofuel crops, and has recently acquired 85,000 hectares of land in Bench Majji Zone in SNNP to establish a rubber plantation.

What exactly are the government's objectives in promoting large-scale agricultural investments and what are the expected benefits to the country? The following goals and benefits are frequently cited in several MOARD documents referred to earlier. Foreign investment will: a) produce export crops and hence increase the country's foreign earnings; it is also expected to expand production of crops needed for agro-industry such as cotton and sugar cane; b) create employment opportunities in the localities concerned; c) benefit local communities through the construction of infrastructure and social assets such as health posts, schools, access to clean water; d) provide the opportunity for technology transfer; and e) promote energy security. We shall see later in the paper that so far there is no evidence that many of these objectives have been met. On the contrary, the evidence we have been able to gather, both through our own field work and those available in written documents, indicates that the damage done at present by the projects outweighs the benefits gained.

Who are the foreign investors that have acquired land and have started operations? The most aggressive investors so far have been Indian companies: at present there are over thirty five firms from that country that have acquired extensive land in various Killils including Beni-Shangul, Gambella and Oromia. This does not include Indian investments in floriculture business, which is considerable. Indian investors as a group hold the largest allotment of land in the country so far (see Tables A1 and A2, for example). Indeed, the government seems to be particularly well disposed to Indian capital and is keenly encouraging it. Several high level missions have visited India to attract investors, and recent local media reports quote Ethiopian officials as saying that about half of the total land earmarked for investment in the GTP in the next five years - about 1.8 million hectares- could be set aside for Indian investors if there is sufficient interest on their part[15]. There has been a dramatic increase in the volume of Indian investment in the country in the last five years[16]. From a lowly figure of about 400 million USD in 2005 it has grown to nearly five billion USD at present. According to Ethiopian government sources, the volume is expected to grow by one billion USD every year. There are now over 500 Indian firms in Ethiopia, and while many of them are in the manufacturing and engineering sectors, a sizable number are engaged in agriculture, particularly food and biofuel production, sugar estates, floriculture and dairy processing. In contrast, China had invested, as of the end of 2009, one billion USD in the country, mostly in manufacturing and construction with only a limited presence in the agricultural sector.

The second most prominent actors in large-scale agriculture are investors from the Middle-East. Sheikh Al-Amoudi and Saudi Star are the largest investors from these countries; Dubai World is involved in a joint venture with a local company to produce tea on a 5,000 hectare estate in Illubabor in Oromia. Many investors from here are engaged in joint ventures with domestic firms, and hence it is not always easy to determine the full extent of their presence in the agricultural sector. Finally, there are a few European and Israeli companies which have large investments, mostly in biofuel production.

---

[15] See for example *Fortune* newspaper 6 February 2011
[16] Based on data reported in government media and the independent press

4.3   Land Deals: Processes and Outcomes

So far there are no established or commonly accepted rules, procedures or guidelines for transfer of land to investors. There are two major channels through which land is provided to investors, namely the Killils and the federal government, through MOARD. While the latter has drafted guidelines for land transfers, rent assessment and land use practices, these have not yet been adopted by the Killils and are not common procedure (see MOARD 2009c,d,e). Even within MOARD, decisions on application for land are made without much regard for the new rules, instead many other considerations are taken into account, including the influence and financial muscle of the investors concerned. The application procedure is fairly simple: investors fill out a standard application form and present a business plan along with their written requests for land. Neither the application form nor the business plan requires stringent commitments or obligations on the part of the investors. Moreover, there are no mechanisms for checking the accuracy of the information provided by investors in these documents, and as a result some investors exaggerate the benefits their project will provide and the capital they hope to invest so as to influence decisions and to gain approval. Once the land to be handed over is determined, the investor is asked to prepare an environmental impact assessment report which is reviewed by MOARD. If the application is given a favorable consideration, which in most cases it is, MOARD instructs the relevant Killil authorities of the case and requests their support and cooperation in facilitating the transfer of land.

In the case of Killils, the Investment Commissions were, until recently, largely responsible for all land deals but now the process involves several Killil bodies. In a good number of cases, earlier applications for land required only the submission of a written request for land by the investor. Frequently, the project land was identified by the investors themselves and recorded in the Commissions' records without any verification or only a cursory one. On a number of occasions, the real size of the land in question would be different from what was shown in the records. In some cases, woreda officials would transfer to the investor less land than was recorded in the contract document if they feared a large number of people would be displaced. The investor signs a contract with the Commissions which then informs the relevant bureaus and woredas to provide support for follow-up and supervision, and to facilitate the transfer of land. However, some Killils, such as Oromia for example, have recently introduced stricter rules and clearer divisions of responsibility. At present, Oromia has given a greater role to its Land and Environmental Protection Bureau in the transfer process, and the latter's responsibilities include identifying the investment land, gathering the necessary land information, reviewing and approving the environmental impact assessment report, and providing periodic follow-up. The task of the Oromia Investment Commission now is to approve the project and sign the contract with the investor. However, in each particular case, once the decision is made, the Killil authorities simply instruct the woreda officials to facilitate the transfer and help in ensuring the implementation of project activities. It is the woreda authorities who have the difficult task of handling any grievances or claims voiced by local households regarding the land in question –and there have been many of these in different parts of the country.

The rental fee charged for agricultural land, which is set out in the land laws of each Killil, varies widely. Most Killils determine the land rent depending on location, access to transport, markets, communication and banking services, and whether the project has access to irrigation water or not. Lands near urban centers and having adequate roads and other basic services and benefitting from an irrigation scheme have the highest rental value. The maximum rent charged, 135 Birr per *hectare* per year, is in Oromia. The following Table shows the maximum and minimum annual rental fees for lands in selected Killils.

Table 2. Rent of Land in Selected Killils (*Birr*/ha/year)

Killil	Maximum	Minimum
Amhara	79.37	14.21
BeniShangul	25.00	15.00
Gambella	30.00	20.00
Oromia	135.00	70.00
SNNP	117.00	30.00
Tigrai	40.00	30.00

SOURCE: Killil legislations (in Dessalegn 2009); findings from field interviews

Rental fees are thus ridiculously low by any standards, indeed one Indian investor who had just been given a sizable chunk of land in the west of the country called them "throw-away prices". In US dollars, investors now pay from $2.00 to less than $10.00 for a hectare of land, while in contrast, rental costs in the Punjab area of India range from Rs 25,000 to 30,000 (556 to 667 USD) per hectare year (*Deccan Herald*, 14 February 2001). Many Indian as well as other foreign investors have been overjoyed by the rates as well as the generous financial incentives they are eligible for, as discuss earlier in this paper. So low are the fees –and this is even recognized by government authorities- that investors are encouraged to request more land than they can possible manage, and many leave the land lie idle for several years as a consequence. The rates are still in place despite the depreciation of the *Birr* against all major currencies and despite growing inflation in the country[17]. There have been suggestions from MOARD and others to increase the rental fee, but many Killils have not yet made any firm decisions on the matter at present. MOARD has recently drafted new guidelines for the determination of rental rates but to the best of my knowledge these have not become standard procedure in the country yet. The new guidelines increase the rates substantially, though it may not be considered high by the standards of other countries. The draft establishes a maximum of 2660 or 2541*Birr* per hectare for irrigated or rain-fed land respectively, located within a 100 km of Addis Ababa, and a minimum of 158 or 111 *Birr* for similar lands located more than 700 km away (MOARD 2009d).

The same document establishes a ceiling for lands to be transferred to investors for various types of crops. A maximum size of 50,000 hectares is set for investors growing biofuel plants, including palm oil trees; those growing cereals, oil seeds or agro-industry crops such as cotton and sugar-cane may request up to 20,000 hectares, while for tea and coffee growers the maximum is set at 5,000. However, these rules are on paper only. According to recent reports in the local media, Saudi Star, a company with a strong Saudi interest, and which acquired 10,000 hectares of land in Gambella in 2008, was recently given permission by MOARD to add another 129,000 hectares to its project in the same Killil to grow rice for export to Saudi Arabia and other countries in the Gulf[18]. The company is in fact seeking a total of 500,000 hectares with 300,000 in Gambella and the rest in Beni Shangul and Oromia. The aim of the company is to get sufficient land to produce one million tons of rice annually for export, and to earn one billion dollars in exports yearly[19].

The lease period for all categories of investment land various among Killils in similar manner. Lands with irrigation have a longer lease period than those without. In a number of Killils (Beni-Shangul, Gambella, SNNP and Tigrai) the lease period extends to 50 years, while in Oromia and Amhara, it is 30 and 25 years respectively. The draft guidelines noted above recommend a lease period of 25 to 45 years, but the author of the document, MOARD itself, has not respected its own recommendations.

---

[17] The *Birr* has been depreciating in value in recent years: in 2009, 1.00 USD was 12.9 Birr, in October 2010, 16.35. The new rental rates suggested by MOARD will have a range of 10 to 160 USD per hectare per year

[18] See the weekly papers *Reporter* (Amharic), and *Fortune*, Sunday 3 October 2010

[19] Interview with acting project manager of the company; press statement in *Reporter* 3 October 2010

As noted earlier, MOARD and the Killil Investment Commissions are responsible for signing contracts with investors. The contract documents are simple and do not demand heavy obligations on the part of investment projects. On the contrary, investors are free to choose what crops to grow and where to market what they have grown, without any interference from their hosts. They are not obliged to supply the local or national market, indeed, they are strongly encouraged to export most or all of their products, as we saw earlier. There are no provisions in the contracts aimed at meeting the food security needs of the country. Moreover, project managers have no contractual obligations to provide social services to the communities concerned or invest in basic infrastructure, on the contrary, in a number of instances it is the government that constructs some of the infrastructure such as roads and irrigations schemes used by the projects. One common item found in almost all Oromia Killil contracts is the obligation of projects to plant native tree species covering at least two percent of project land; federal contracts do not have such obligations but require projects to "conserve tree plantations that have not been cleared for earth works" –a vague clause that is of little benefit. The environmental impact assessment conducted by the projects as part of their successful acquisition of land is also meant to ensure that land management practices employed by them do not damage the environment and the land. However, the clearing of woody and herbaceous vegetation that projects are undertaking at present, and the resultant loss of vegetation cover is exposing lands in several Killils to serious erosion and land degradation, and depriving local populations of valuable natural resources (I shall return to this later).

The responsibility for monitoring and oversight, and the task of enforcing project obligations is placed on the shoulders of Killil offices and staff, however all the officials concerned we were able to interview readily admit that there very little institutional and technical capacity to carry out these tasks effectively. In some of the Killils the responsibility is entrusted to the land and environmental protection units, in others it is the Investment Commissions, supported by the bureaus of agriculture. In MOARD, there is a unit that has been charged with similar tasks but was established only recently and has severe capacity constraints and very limited outreach. The projects are spread out throughout the country and the Killils and cover great distances which makes it extremely difficult to carry out periodic visits for on-site inspection and monitoring by staff who are already burdened with numerous other duties.

Equally significant are the inter-agency contradictions and the lack of consultation in decision making. Criticisms of the Investment Commissions for poor management and lack of capacity by the Killil land and environment or agricultural bureaus is not uncommon. One agency is often unaware of decisions made by another until it is informed of the need for its involvement after many measures have already been taken. At the federal level it is MOARD which makes all the decisions but key agencies such as, for instance, the Ethiopian Wildlife Conservation Authority (EWCA), which is responsible for managing the country's national parks, game reserves and sanctuaries, and which may be affected by decisions taken, are often not consulted. EWCA was not aware, for example, of the decision to transfer hundreds of thousands of hectares of lands in the middle of the Gambella national park or the Babile elephant sanctuary in the east of Oromia to investors until environmental and conservation groups raised the alarm and took the matter to the authorities concerned[20].

The interagency contradictions are aggravated by the contradictions inherent in the land transfer program itself. Here is a program that has indiscriminately given out huge tracts of land to foreign investors, in great haste and inadequate preparation and limited information, and without consultation with the people and local public officials directly affected by it. Land that has been transferred includes arable land, land used for grazing, woodland, forest land, savanna grassland, and wetlands. There have been at least two notable cases, one in Gambella and the other in the east of Oromia, where land inside a formally designated national park, protected area and wildlife sanctuary was given to investors. The enclosure of the land, vegetation clearing and farm operation has had, or will soon have, a damaging impact on land resources, wildlife, bio-diversity, water sources and the natural environment. The damage to people's livelihoods is beginning to be evident in many ways: it has led to loss of farm land, of pasturage and grazing rights, of sources of water, and the loss of access to firewood and useful plants.

There have been several incidents of protest by peasants in several parts of the country, some robust but many low-key and subdued. Of the latter kind are peasant encroachments on land given out to investment projects, driving livestock to graze on them, disputing boundary limits, taking one's grievances to court, or appealing to higher authorities for redress of grievances. The more robust ones have involved community agitations and group action. In some instances, even local officials have voiced their reservations or discontent over the land deals they have been asked to implement by their superiors (Ensermu et al 2009, Gizachew and Solomon 2010). Group action and demonstrations have occurred in Gambella and Bako woreda, where we have done field work, in which peasants contested the transfer of land and attempted to drive off the project staff. In Bako, the federal police had to be called in to put down the demonstration and to restore order.

---

[20] For the environmentalists struggle over the Babille elephant sanctuary see Ensermu et al 2009, and Heckett and Negussu 2008

5.   Findings from Gambella Killil and Bako Tibee Woreda

We undertook field work in two areas in the country, where we gathered first hand information and conducted extended interviews with farming people, local officials, employees of investment projects and other concerned persons. The two are Gambella in the extreme west of the country, and Bako Tibee woreda located in western Oromia. In what follows I shall discuss the findings of our field work and the impact of the land deals on people's livelihoods.

5.1   Gambella

Gambella has been, and still is one of the Killils which has attracted considerable investor attention and has been targeted as focal area for land investments by MOARD as well as other government agencies on account of what is perceived to be its extensive and untapped land and water resources. Domestic investors began to acquire land here even before the investment legislation noted above was issued and before the government had given the green light to large-scale investments. Data from the Killil's Investment Commission shows that there are now numerous large-scale investors, both domestic and foreign, and the total land transferred to them at present may reach over 300,000 hectares (see Table A3 in Annex 1 for a partial list of large investors).There are also numerous medium and small-sized investments (with land measuring from 500 to less than 2000 hectares) scattered throughout Gambella, but there was not much information available on them at the time of our field work. The Investment Commission, which is responsible for maintaining an accurate database, was unable to provide full information on the investment program in the Killil. Nevertheless we estimate from all available records and oral information obtained that the total land held by all investors, small, medium and large, had reached about 500,000 hectares by the end of 2010. More land will be given out to investors in the months ahead as the Killil administration as well as the federal government are keen to attract investors to Gambella which is said to possess 1.2 million hectares of unused land suitable for investment. As the field work for this study was underway there was local press reports that Saudi Star, a company which already has 10,000 hectares of land in Abobo woreda, one of the well endowed woredas of Gambella, and the use of the Alwero dam, had submitted a request for 129,000 hectares of additional land for its rice project there. The request, it was said, was approved by the government and the company had been asked to submit a detailed business plan for it. The company's plans are to acquire a total of 300,000 hectares in Gambella to grow rice for export to Saudi Arabia (*Reporter*, Amharic, 3 October 2010)[21].

The main interest of the large projects here is growing high value export commodities such as rice, soya beans and other pulses, and sesame; bio-fuel plants such as palm-oil trees are also attracting a good deal of interest. Some investors are planning to grow maize as a second or third crop but this is largely for bio-fuel purposes rather than as food for the local market. Except for two companies, all other investors have a lease period of 50 years, and almost all have been committed to pay a rental fee of 30 to 35 *Birr* (less than two USD) per hectare per year (depending on the use of irrigation water). Many of the small investors are engaged in growing oil seeds, cotton, maize, peanuts and fruit trees. All investment projects, small or large, will require secure access to sources of water for irrigation without which many of them will not be sustainable.

Gambella is located in the extreme west of the country and shares a long border as well as many ecological features with southern Sudan. While in population terms it is relatively sparsely settled (less than half a million inhabitants), the Killil nevertheless has a unique ecology and is immensely rich in biodiversity and wildlife[22]. The land cover consists of several varieties of woodland, high forest, shrub-land, savanna grassland and permanent and seasonal wetlands; the largest permanent wetland in the country is located here. There are four rivers that flow through it, three of which (Akobo, Baro and Gilo) feed into the Sobat River in the Sudan which forms an important tributary of the White Nile. The fourth river, Alwero, has a dam built over it and provides irrigation water for Saudi Star, the second largest investor in the Killil. Local inhabitants use the rivers to catch fish which is a useful income earner for families as well as being consumed at home. Gambella was neglected for many decades under the two previous regimes and is thus not well endowed in basic infrastructure and services.

One of the most important "hidden treasures" of Gambella is its diverse wildlife. There are some twenty or so important wild animal species in the area of which several are of international significance. There is an immense wildlife migration that takes place seasonally between Gambella and the Sudan, and experts believe that this is the *second largest wildlife migration* in the world, after that of the Serengeti in east Africa[23]. The major animal species are the white-eared kob,

---

[21] In an interview I had at the end of August 2010 with the acting manager of the company's Gambella rice project I was informed that Saudi Star had submitted an application for 125,000 hectares of land in Gambella.

[22] What follows is based on TFCI 2010a,b, and findings from our field work

[23] A video film produced for TFCI Task Force by John Purdie (2010) on Gambella's hidden treasure is visually impressive.

Nile lechwe, hartebeest, roan antelope, giraffe, buffalo, warthog, water buck, and elephant. There is also a diversity of birdlife along the rivers and in the wetlands. The population of the white-eared kob is estimated to be about 750,000 of which some 255,000 make their habitat in Gambella while the rest are in the Sudan. The Nile lechwe is a rare animal found only in the Sudan and Gambella, and is now on the endangered list of the world conservation body, IUCN. The wildlife species are distributed throughout the western half of Gambella and along the entire border with the Sudan. Many of the animals in question engage in short-distance seasonal migration within the Killil also, moving from one ecology to another in the dry and wet seasons in search of food, water and change of habitat. The Killil has one national park and several protected areas. The Gambella National Park was established in 1974 but was neither gazetted nor effectively managed for many years.

Gambella is inhabited by several ethnic minority groups of which the three major ones are the Annuak, (population 100,000), the Nuer (113,000), and, the numerically smaller of the three, the Majangir (60,000) who live in the south-western part of the Killil adjacent to the SNNP. The customary system of property relations among all three groups is founded on communal ownership, and for this, and other reasons that we need not discuss here, land certification and registration was not undertaken in Gambella. For each of the three ethnic groups, the land, the natural resources and the ecosystem in place are vital for their livelihood, however, all of them have now been affected, in varying degrees, by the large number of investment projects that have sprung up all over in the last five to six years. These projects are seen as a threat by many as we found out in our field visit and as will be discussed further down.

The Annuaks, who live in dispersed settlements, are dependent on the cultivation of the land and crop production (maize, sorghum, sweet potato and ground-nuts), but they supplement their income with fishing on the banks of the river, with hunting (as a source for meat), honey production, and access to a wide variety of resources from the woodlands, forests and grasslands around them. Cultivation here is based on the hoe and hand tools, and most of the time what is produced is not enough for the needs of families the whole year round. Frequently therefore, the period from January to May is the hardship season, and April to May are the difficult and hungry months. Conditions are worse if a drought occurs, as happened in 2008 and 2009, and in such circumstances people may be reduced to starvation. However, families depend on wild food sources collected from the woods and forests of their surroundings to live through the hardship season. The Annuaks thus eke out a precarious existence and depend greatly on the ecosystem and surrounding natural resources for their survival.

The Nuer on the other hand are pastoralists and transhumance cultivators, meaning they move from the banks of the rivers to the uplands and vice versa, depending on the seasons and the flooding of the rivers. The rivers flood the plains during the rainy season which is from June through August, at which time the Nuer and their livestock move to live in the upper woodland areas and cultivate crops for the season. At the end of the flood period, in October/November, they return with their livestock down to the banks of the rivers and stay there up to May to herd their animals and cultivate crops on land enriched by the floods. Thus for the Nuer the rivers are vital for their sustenance as well as the survival of their livestock. The Majangir inhabit the area which is the most densely forested in the Killil and they too depend on forest resources for their livelihood. They are particularly noted as honey producers for which the forest ecosystem is critical. Moreover, for all population groups the ecosystem provides a variety of other essential resources, including wood for tools, grass for homesteads, wild food, medicinal and other useful plants, and access to water resources.

It is against this background that we should examine the transfer of large tracts of land to investors in Gambella. The investments underway are to be found in many parts of the Killil, and some are inside the National Park and protected areas, or inside the established habitats of many of the wildlife. Others have been established in areas which effectively block or interfere with transit corridors, and the migration routes of the animals, and yet others are in locations which will deprive the animals of access to seasonal pastures or water points. So far there have not been significant evictions of individual land holders (though, as will be noted further down, evictions in the form of mass resettlement is now underway), but humans populations have been affected because the projects are depriving them of vital resources from what until now was their common property. Moreover, the clearing of the land by investment projects and the loss of the woods, grass and other vegetation is causing hardship to the local communities as we found out in our field work.

Our field work was undertaken among the Annuak population in two villages in Abobo woreda, which, as indicated in Annex 1, Table A3, has been the center of investment activity in the last five years. The villages we had chosen, each containing 90 and 120 households, were directly affected by the establishment of the Saudi Star investment project which was given rights to use the Alwero River and the waters of the dam built during the Derg. At the time of our field visit the Killil had launched a full-scale resettlement program aimed at moving populations in all parts of the territory to settlements sites designated by the authorities[24]. The program was a complete surprise to the villagers we

---

[24] Initially the program was called a resettlement program, but now has designated as villagization

interviewed, all of whom informed our team that they had no knowledge of it and were not consulted. The justification given by the authorities was that resettlement would give public agents better access to communities enabling them to provide essential services such as health, education and clean water. Resettlement is also said to make it easier for government to plan and deliver agricultural extension programs, and to better protect communities from periodic natural hazards such as floods, forest fires and storms. However, the villagers we interviewed were not convinced these were the main reasons for the resettlement program, noting that if this was the case public agents could have provided the services to them in their present locations without the need for relocation. The program was in fact bitterly resented by the people in the two communities as well by other Annuak cultivators we interviewed informally when we met them by chance. Everyone was convinced that this was meant to clear the land for the investment projects in place as well as those planned in the future. The people called it a "clearance program" and what they were offered in return were settlement sites which they said were unsuitable for habitation and cultivation. Public officials our team interviewed insisted that the program was initiated earlier and was not connected with the investment program but did concede that its original objective was subverted in subsequent decisions. There is reason to believe that the relocation program was most likely suggested but quite certainly approved by the federal government because Gambella received a large fund from the central treasury to implement the program. It is worth noting here that as this paper was being written there were reports in the government-controlled media that another Killil, Beni-Shangul, which has also been the focus of investment activity similar to Gambella, was undertaking a similar resettlement program.

Many Annuaks interviewed said the land given to the investment project belongs to the community, though some were of the opinion that it belonged to the state because no one paid any tax on it. All were agreed, however, that it was transferred to investors without their knowledge or consent, and without any compensation paid to their communities. They considered the land and the resources on it common property and feared that the loss of these resources would deprive them of essential means of livelihood. Community people were informed of the land transfer by woreda officials who tried to convince them that the transfer would be of great benefit to the communities. On the other hand, the officials interviewed stated that they themselves were not consulted on the matter and were only instructed by authorities higher up to convey the decision to the people concerned. One official told our team that he was at first positive about the investment project but now is having second thoughts. There were many promises of support to the communities by higher officials and project management but none of these promises, he said, were kept.

Most community residents were not convinced that anything good will come out of the transfer of their land to outsiders, though a few of our interviewees did say they had positive expectations initially but not any longer. Everyone is now anxious that the clearing of the land by Saudi Star, and the large-scale deforestation this has caused, will bring social and economic hardship and that wildlife which used to be plentiful in the area, and which they hunted occasionally for consumption, have now disappeared. Even the local officials interviewed saw little benefit to the residents of the two villages; indeed, they expressed dissatisfaction that what was produced by the project was destined for export and that there would be nothing left to benefit the local market. Gambella is not self-sufficient in food and as noted above there are several months in the year when there are food shortages. Because the Alwero dam has been ceded to Saudi Star, community people, especially the women, are fearful that they will soon be denied access to their fishing rights and there would be shortage of water in the future. Respondents informed our team that the project has not provided any services or invested in any assets of benefit to the community.

The following quote from the response of one of the women interviewed by our team expresses the general sentiment of many, and especially of women, in the community

> …Two years ago, for example, there was a severe shortage of maize because of the drought. We managed to survive the hunger that ensued because we were able to collect roots and other edible plants from the forest. We were able to eat because of the forest. Since the forest has been cleared, I do not know what we are going to eat if there is another food shortage. When there is food shortage it is we women and our children who suffer most because the men go to the towns to look for daily labor. In the past we depended on the forest to get food but now that the forest has been cleared I fear that our children will die of starvation. Another thing, …in the future the private investors may ask us to buy the wood and grass that we used to get from the forest for free. In our tradition it is women who collect grass for house building, but now there is shortage of grass [because of the clearance by the project] and wood is also scarce; the men bring the wood from long distances. … They say the river will be diverted for the benefit of the project farm, if this is the case, we will be confronted with water shortage, and also fish will disappear. … Therefore we are not happy with the coming of the project. In brief the investors will not provide any benefits to us, they have come for their own interest. [Aryat Oujolu, Turkodi sub-Kebelle]

On the other hand, a number of interviewees saw the employment opportunities provided by the project as a positive thing. However, almost all the unskilled manual and seasonal jobs were taken up by local people while the skill operators were people from other parts of the country. There was no job security nor any program of training or upgrading provided. Wage rates were low, ranging from 17 to 23 Birr per day. According to interviews we had with a senior manager of

Saudi Star in Addis Ababa, the project employs on the average 250 workers of which between 50 to 60 are skilled and permanent employees and the rest daily laborers from the local population.

Finally a brief discussion of a protest conducted by communities in Godere woreda in response to the allocation of forest land to an Indian investor is instructive[25]. Godere woreda in the extreme south of Gambella is inhabited by the Majangir and another ethnic group; it is adjacent to the SNNP, with which it shares similarities in ecology and ethnic composition -the same ethnic groups are to be found on both sides of the border. The woreda is highly forested and many here depend on the forest for their livelihoods, and especially so because honey production is an important economic activity. Communities here have a unique form of rights to trees on which bee hives are hang, which everyone respects. In essence the forest is common property in which individuals hold rights over the trees their hives are placed.

In the past, investors had cleared the forest on the SNNP side of the border for planting tea and the people of Godere were aware of the hardships caused to the local inhabitants. So when the communities in Godere heard that an Indian company called Lucky Exports had been granted 5000 hectares of prime forest land to establish a tea plantation it became clear to them that their traditional ways of life would be threatened if not destroyed. They thus organized a series of proactive meetings to discuss the matter and resolved to take their case to the federal government since they were suspicious that the local authorities were complicit in the investment decision. The meetings were held without the knowledge of the woreda authorities. According to evidence we gathered from protestors, who for understandable reasons did not wish to give their names, the protest leaders are reported to have prepared an alternative land-use plan which involved the transfer of the land given to the investor to the community to use it to grow agricultural products without disturbing the forest or damaging the ecosystem; they believed their plan would protect the forest ecology and also be an important measure to reduce youth unemployment. They were able to send an envoy to Addis Ababa to take the case to the country's President who in turn expressed his deep concern in a written letter to EPA. The authorities here wrote a strong letter to MOARD protesting the transfer of forest land to an investor and echoing the concerns of the communities concerned. The contents of the letter along with a brief report on the case subsequently appeared in the local press. The President, who is well known for his keen environmental interest, is reported to have written to the protestors supporting their demand for the protection of the forest. At the time of our field work the investor in question had

---

[25] Based on field interviews, and the weekly newspaper *Reporter* 12 May 2010. See also Zelalem 2009

refrained from clearing the land and left the area hoping to start activities at a later date when the agitations had died down. Right now, as these lines are being written, there is a standoff and the forest has been saved for the time being, but the local authorities have detained a number of activists suspected of being protest leaders.

5.2 Bako Tibee Woreda

Bako Tibee woreda, located in West Shoa Zone is about 250 kms west of Addis Ababa. It is in Oromia and inhabited predominantly by the Oromo people. Just as in other parts of the country, the majority of people here are peasant farmers dependent on family plots as well as resources from common lands in the surrounding environment. The woreda has twenty-eight kebelles, with a total population of 125,000 inhabitants. The land cover consists of arable land, grazing land, open wood land, forest and shrub land. Over half of the woreda lies in the *qolla* (low altitude) agro-ecology, and nearly 40 percent in the *woyna degga* (mid-altitude) zone. The woreda is relatively well endowed with water resources: it is covered by several small rivers, numerous permanent and seasonal streams and springs, and is bounded on the south by the Gibe River which is one of the largest tributaries of the Omo River. The major crops grown are maize, sorghum, wheat, teff, oil seeds and spices. Because of the agro-ecology and the relatively large extent of grazing land available, livestock raising is an important income earner and there is a large livestock population. Farming communities here distinguish between two types of land based on their soil properties: one is called black soil or *koticha* land, and the other red soil land. The *koticha* land in Bechera Oda Gibe kebelle, the site of our study, was used both for grazing and farming purposes, whereas the red soil land is predominantly farming land.

The woreda has so far attracted three large-scale investors, one domestic and two foreign ones, but more are expected to arrive in the future. The domestic investor, United Farm Business, was recently allotted 3000 hectares of land in Oda Gibe Kebelle, located to the south of the kebelle where we did our field interviews. This was the company that was the object of a strong community protest noted earlier in this paper. The largest foreign investor is Karuturi, the same Indian firm operating in Gambella, while at the time of our field work, a second Indian company was visiting a kebelle located in the west of the woreda to see the land it was promised by the Killill authorities.

Our findings from Bako are broadly similar to those in Gambella though there are some significant differences. Bako is not endowed with the kind of wildlife and biodiversity that was such an important feature of Gambella, and similarly there was no resettlement program either. On the other hand, just as in Gambella, peasants as well as local officials here were not consulted in the decision to transfer the land to Karuturi or the other investors. This Indian company which already had received an enormous estate in Gambella was allotted 11,000 hectares in Bako in 2009, with the bulk of its holdings lying in Bechera Oda Gibe kebelle which stretched to the Gibe River. Its plans are to grow rice, palm oil trees and maize, destined predominantly for export. Right now it is not operating all the land under its control but will soon cover all of it as it expands its operations. It has been allowed to make use of a relatively large river in the vicinity called the Abuko River which flows into the Gibe. Local farmers used to depend on the river to grow sugar cane and vegetables along its banks but the river as well as other streams and natural springs are no longer accessible to them because they are now being utilized by the project.

The land transferred to the Karuturi is predominantly *koticha* land, which in the distant past was under the ownership of a succession of local gentry but in recent times, and especially under the reforms of the Derg, was considered common property. Even in the past, under gentry ownership, the bulk of the *koticha* was used for grazing by the community as well as households further afield. This custom was maintained right to the present day until the land was transferred to the project. Over the years, plots of koticha land adjacent to human settlements had been used by peasants to grow a variety of food crops. Moreover, peasants interviewed stressed that the koticha land was used for other important purposes by the community: it provided access to firewood, to useful plants and water sources both for humans and livestock, and served as a setting for holding community and cultural events. It was thus by no means "unused" land as the Killil authorities claimed: there was in fact a strong sense of community rights to the land among all the peasants interviewed for our study. However, neither the pasture field nor the plots in it farmed by neighboring peasants was registered by the authorities during the land certification program in 2008, indicating that higher authorities in the Oromia had decided much earlier to set the land aside for large-scale investment. Peasants who had farming plots in the land were denied certification of their plots and thus were not eligible for compensation when the land was taken by the investor.

This was one of the causes of resentment by peasants directed against both the woreda and Killil authorities as well as Karuturi. Peasants interviewed believed they were entitled to have their plots in koticha registered as they had been farming the land for many years with the tacit approval of the local authorities. When the land was transferred to the investor, some 500 peasants lost their plots here. Peasants also resented the destruction of the natural vegetation caused by the clearance of the land undertaken by the project and the uprooting of old and much valued trees. The black soil was covered with open woodland and some of the trees, especially *ficus sycomorus*[26] were valued by the community for religio-cultural reasons. These imposing trees have symbolic meaning in Oromo culture and are revered by rural Oromo communities. They provide shade for humans and livestock, are used as venues for community gatherings and peace-making, and have religious significance.

The company had not made any significant infrastructural or social investments in the area except to repair and widen an old dirt track leading from the main road to the project site, and to provide some plastic sheeting to a community school some distance from the project site. In the process of extending the road many people close by lost their fruit trees and some land but they were denied compensation. When some of the people concerned protested to the woreda authorities they were put in detention and only released some ten days later after being given severe warnings not to "cause trouble". According to informants some 150 peasants lost property, including registered plots, during the extension of the dirt road but were denied compensation. Peasants complained that the loss of their common and individual property has brought hardship and reduced their income.

The project has provided some employment to people in Bechera Oda and other adjacent kebelles, however the majority of employees are casual laborers with little or no employment security and no benefits other than the daily wage they receive. Wage laborers and others interviewed were not particularly well disposed to the project, some were even hostile because they felt they were unfairly treated, had no job security and not infrequently abused. Two women laborers told our team that they had suffer physical abuse and sexual harassment at work. The Indian project staff (there is one Indian site manager and ten Indian employees) are said to look down upon local employees including their skilled workers. The project pays a daily wage of 12 Birr to its casual work force, which is lower than what peasants working in the Productive Safety Net Program (PSNP) earn in a day[27]. The permanent employees number about 30 while there are some 60 regular non-skill laborers. The number of casual workers varies according to the work schedule and the season: in the peak season, the number may reach over 600, but otherwise the average number does not exceed 200. In times of high demand, the project uses a rotational employment method, that is, each week new laborers are selected to work on the field and laborers that had worked the previous week are let go. This is one of the causes of discontent because working for the project under this scheme does not earn them much

---

[26] The local name in the Oromo language is *oda*, (Amharic *sholla)*; the English name is sycamore fig. Some of the names of kebelles in the woreda have "Oda" attached to them indicating how common the tree was here.

[27] The PSNP is a multi-donor supported program which provides employment (or direct assistance) to food insecure households, and pays from 16 to 18 Birr per day for casual labor.

income. For all employees there is no employment security nor any means of wage upgrading based on experience gained and longer service. While a few of the permanent employees are able to operate some of the farm machinery with a bit of training, there are no training or upgrading programs set up by the project. In sum, there is clear evidence that the project is unpopular in the woreda and many of the people in the community are resentful of the special favors they believe has been given to it by the government.

6. Conclusions

The agricultural investment program eagerly promoted by the government has far-reaching socio-economic and political implications and it is thus important that there is informed debate on the subject within civil society and among concerned citizens and the public in this country. To begin with, the government has already transferred about 3.5 million hectares of land to investors and is now taking measures to transfer a similar amount in the next five years. By the end of 2015, the country's agrarian structure will have been changed significantly, and the shift from small-scale to large-scale farming, dominated by foreign capital and enjoying privileged status, will pose a serious threat to the long-term sustainability of the rural economy, the livelihoods of peasants and pastoralists, and to the goals of achieving food security. The new agricultural system will progressively marginalize smallholders, creating in the process unequal and antagonistic social classes (those privileged by the program and those disadvantaged by it), and producing a wide gulf between the haves and have-nots. Capitalist investors, particularly foreign ones will be driven solely by the profit motive and the need to supply the export market, and this will mean adopting systems of land management (industrial forms of mono-cropping, for example) which will not be environment-friendly and which will in the long run leave the land and the ecosystem exhausted and unusable by future generations. As was shown above, the land deals that have been concluded so far provide no adequate safeguards, neither do government institutions have the capacity for effective monitoring of project activities. Investors have been given a virtual free hand and are bound by few enforceable obligations.

Secondly, the state has used its hegemonic authority over the land to dispossess smallholders and their communities without consultation or consent. In most cases, the land deals lacked transparency and accountability hence they have had the effect of eroding confidence and trust among the people and their communities. The loss of property does not only bring economic and social deprivation but also a sense of insecurity and the loss of voice. Thirdly, there are no formal or informal obligations on the part of investment projects to contribute to the food security needs of the country. The contracts signed by investors and the business plans approved do not contain provisions requiring projects to supply the local market, whether as a matter of course or under emergency circumstances. As has been noted above, there is a strong food security element in the on-going global rush for land, particularly in Africa, though we should not ignore the opportunity for high profits to be gained by investors planning to export to the world market at a time when food prices are relative high, as they have been in recent years, and as they are expected to remain for a long while. One of the reasons why Gulf country investors are keen to acquire land in Africa and Ethiopia is to be able to grow food crops for export to their home markets to ensure food security for their populations. On the other hand, Indian companies are rushing to acquire land in Ethiopia partly for their own country's food needs and partly for the export market. It is thus paradoxical that the government of one of the most vulnerable countries in the world is handing over vast land and water resources to foreign investors to help the food security efforts of their home countries, or to gain profits for their companies, without making adequate safeguards and without taking into account the food security needs of its own people.

Fourthly, the government's objectives in promoting large-scale investments have to a large extent not been met, nor are some of them likely to be met in the present circumstances. There is, for example, hardly any technology transfer at the moment. The projects are operated with high technology which is not transferrable or affordable to smallholders. Indeed, large-scale agriculture is managed quite differently from family farms, and there is no meeting ground between the two under the present policy environment. As we found out, and as has been suggested in some preliminary works that have already appeared[28], many projects have made hardly any social investments for the benefit of the communities around them. Moreover, since foreign investors are allowed to raise up to 70 percent of their operational costs from local sources, and since their export earnings may either be transferred to their home accounts or repatriated fully, it is difficult to see how the government is expected to gain much hard currency. Furthermore, the disproportionate favor shown to foreign capital is counter-productive because it creates roadblocks against the growth of a vigorous local entrepreneurial class, and, in the long run, is bound to lead to national as well as economic dependency. Experience in other countries has shown that under proper regulation, domestic capital is more likely to act in ways that are socially responsible than its foreign counterpart.

Finally, the government has not given sufficient consideration to different land-use options but has instead blindly put its faith on large-scale farming. There are a variety of sound land-use options that have been tried successfully in Africa and elsewhere which have been high foreign currency earners and also beneficial to local communities but without posing a serious threat to the environment and natural resources. In the case of Gambella, for example, experts now in the field have suggested that if its extensive wildlife resources are properly managed and conserved they could provide immense economic and social benefit to the people and the Killil and create high employment opportunities through a variety of sustainable schemes that do not damage the ecosystem and the wildlife but on the contrary preserve and support them (TFCI 2009). Such schemes include ecotourism, game ranching, controlled hunting, fishing, income from

---

[28] Ensermu et al 2009; Hecket and Negusu 2008

conservation-based schemes such as REDD, and improved livestock production programs. Experts even think that Gambella could be eligible for a world heritage status for its incredibly rich wildlife but, unfortunately, this is now seriously threatened by ill-conceived agricultural investment programs.

References

- ***Publications***

Borras Jr. S M and Jennifer Franco 2010. Towards a Broader View of the Politics of Global Land Grab. Rethinking Land Issues, Reframing Resistance. ICAS Working Paper Series No. 001. Initiatives in Critical Agrarian Studies, Land Deals Politics Institute and Transnational Institute. Accessed by web search

Cotula, L, S. Vermeulen, R. Leonard and J. Keely 2009. *Land Grab or Development Opportunity? Agricultural Investment and International Land Deals in Africa*, London: IIED and FAO

Dessalegn Rahmato 2003. *Resettlement in Ethiopia: The Tragedy of Population Relocation in the 1980s*. FSS Discussion Paper No. 11, Forum for Social Studies, Addis Ababa

_____2009. *The Peasant and the State: Studies in Agrarian Change in Ethiopia 1950s – 2000s*. Addis Ababa: Addis Ababa University Press

_____2010a. Globalization and Food Security: Can Ethiopia Meet the Challenge? Paper prepared for the International Conference on the Ethiopian Economy, Ethiopian Economic Association, Addis Ababa, June

_____2010b. Civil Society and the State: The Challenge of Democratization in Ethiopia. In B. Moyo and G. Machel, eds, *(Dis)Enabling the Public Sphere: Civil Society Regulation in Africa (Volume 1)*. Midrand: South Africa Trust and Trust Africa.

Ensermu Kelbessa, Negusu Aklilu and Tadesse Woldemariam (eds) 2009. Agrofuel Development in Ethiopia: Findings of an Assessment. Addis Ababa, Forum for Environment.

Federal Democratic Republic of Ethiopia (FDRE) 2002a. Re-Enactment of the Investment Proclamation. Proclamation No. 280, *Negarit Gazeta*, Addis Ababa, July

_____2002b. Environmental Protection Organs Establishment Proclamation. Proclamation No. 295, *Federal Negarit Gazeta*, Addis Ababa, October

_____2002c. Environmental Impact Assessment Proclamation. Proclamation No. 299, *Federal Negarit Gazeta*, Addis Ababa, December

_____2003a. A Proclamation to Amend the Investment Re-Enactment Proclamation No. 280/2002. Proclamation No. 375, *Federal Negarit Gazeta*, Addis Ababa, October

_____2005 Rural Land Administration and Land Use Proclamation. Proclamation No. 456, *Federal Negarit Gazeta*, Addis Ababa, July

_____2007. The Struggle to Build a Democratic System and Revolutionary Democracy [Amharic]. Addis Ababa, March

_____2008a. Ethiopian Wildlife Development and Conservation Authority Establishment Proclamation. Proclamation No. 575, Federal Negarit Gazeta, Addis Ababa, May

_____2003b. Council of Ministers Regulation on Investment Incentives and Investment Areas Reserved for Domestic Investors. Regulation No. 84, Federal Negarit Gazeta, Addis Ababa, February

_____2008b. Council of Ministers Regulation to Amend the Investment Incentives and Investment Areas Reserved for Domestic Investors Regulation. Regulation No. 146, Federal Negarit Gazeta, Addis Ababa, March

_____2009. Council of Ministers Regulation to Provide for Wildlife Development, Conservation and Utilization. Regulation No. 163, Federal Negarit Gazeta, Addis Ababa, February

_____2010. Council of Ministers Directive regarding the Administration of Agricultural Investment Land. [Unpublished], Addis Ababa, March

FAO 2010. Eastern and Anglophone Western Africa Regional Assessment: FAO Voluntary Guidelines on Responsible Governance of Tenure of Land and Other Natural Resources, Addis Ababa, Ethiopia, 20-22 September, 2010

Gizachew Abegaz and Solomon Bekure (eds) 2010. *Rural Land Transactions and Agricultural Investment. Proceedings of a Consultative Meeting, Adama 15-17 June 2009.* Addis Ababa: ELAP (Ethiopia Land Administration Program)

GRAIN 2008. Seized: The 2008 Land Grab for Food and Financial Security. www.grain.org

Green Forum 2010. Green Power: Sustainable Energy for Ethiopia. Ensuring Energy Security in a Changing Climate. Proceedings of the 4th Green Forum Conference, Addis Ababa, 1-2 October 2009. Addis Ababa, Green Forum

Hall, Ruth 2010. The Many Faces of the Investor Rush in Southern Africa: Towards a Typology of Commercial Land Deals. Unpublished paper, courtesy of the author

Heckett, Tibebwa and Negusu Aklilu (eds) 2008. *Agrofuel Development in Ethiopia: Rhetoric, Reality and Recommendations*. Addis Ababa: Forum for Environment

Imeru Tamrat 2010. Governance of Large Scale Agricultural Investments in Africa: The Case of Ethiopia. Paper presented at the World Bank Conference on Land Policy and Administration, Washington, D.C., April

IFPRI 2009. "Land Grabbing" by Foreign Investors in Developing Countries: Risks and Opportunities. J. von Braun and Ruth Meinzen-Dick. IFPRI Policy Brief 12, Washington, D.C., April

Investment Agency 2009. Summary Sector, Sub-sector & Division Investment Projects Investment & status since 1992 –December 31, 2009 G.C. Addis Ababa

Mathieu, Paul 2009. Global Investment in Agriculture and Large-scale Land Acquisitions: Risks, Opportunities and Implications for Rural Development. Presentation at MOFA, The Hague, December 16

MELCA Mahiber 2008. Rapid Assessment of Biofuels Development Status in Ethiopia and Proceedings of the National Workshop on Environmental Impact Assessment and Biofuels. Addis Ababa, September

Ministry of Agriculture and Rural Development (MOARD) 2008. Agricultural Investment Potential of Ethiopia. Addis Ababa, November (www.moard.gov.et)

_____ 2009a. List of Investment Projects in Agriculture Sector from July 1992 – February 6, 2009 (Compiled from Killil investment data), Addis Ababa

_____ 2009b. Guideline for Agricultural Project/Business Planning. Addis Ababa, February (www.moard.gov.et)

_____ 2009c. Planned System for Administration of Investment Land [Amharic]. Addis Ababa, June

_____ 2009d. Directives for Implementation of Rental Fees for Agricultural Investment Land [Amharic]. Addis Ababa, December

_____ 2009e. Revised Directive for the Implementation of Agricultural Investment Land Use Follow-up and Support. Addis Ababa

_____ 2010a. General Brushure [sic]. Addis Ababa, March (www.moard.gov.et)

_____ 2010b. Environmental Code of Practice for Agricultural Investment [Draft]. Addis Ababa, June.

Ministry of Finance and Economic Development (MOFED) 2003. Rural Development Policy and Strategies. Addis Ababa, April

_____2006. Ethiopia: Building Progress: A Plan for Accelerated and Sustained Development to End Poverty (PASDEP). Addis Ababa, September.

_____2010a. Updated 2nd PASDEP Agric. Sec. Plan (2003- 2007) [2011-2015]. PDF file.

_____2010b. PASDEP – 2011 Plan. Final. PDF file

_____2010c. Implementation of First Five Year Development Pland (1998-20002[Eth. C]), and Preparation of Next Five Year Plan for Growth and Transformation (2003-2007 [Eth. C]) [Amharic]. [Power Point presentation]. Addis Ababa, July

Ministry of Mines and Energy (MME) 2007. The Biofuel Development and Utilization Strategy of Ethiopia. Addis Ababa, September

The Oakland Institute 2009. The Great Land Grab. Rush for World's Farmland Threatens Food Security for the Poor. By S. Daniel with A. Mittal. www.oaklandinstitute.org

Schoneveld, G.C., Laura A German, and E. Nutakor 2010. Paper Summary – Towards Sustainable Biofuel Development: Assessing the Local Impacts of Large-Scale Foreign Land Acquisitions in Ghana. Unpublished summary of paper.

Taye Assefa (ed) 2008. *Digest of Ethiopia's National Policies, Strategies and Programs*. Addis Ababa: Forum for Social Studies

Trans-Frontier Conservation Initiative (TFCI) Task Force 2010a. Prospecting the Omo-Gambella Landscape for the Establishment of a Network of Protected Areas. Power point presentation by Sanne van Aarst, Parks and Buffer Zones Management Programme, Addis Ababa

_____2010b. Aerial Survey Report: Gambella Reconnaissance 2009 & Census 2010. Draft report, Addis Ababa

Woody Biomass Inventory and Strategic Planning Project (WBISPP) 2004. Forest Resources of Ethiopia. Addis Ababa, May

World Bank 2009. Securing Land Tenure and Improving Livelihoods: Towards a set of Principles for Responsible Agro-investment. Draft Paper for Discussion. Washington, D.C. September 21

_____2010. *Rising Global Interest in Farmland. Can It Yield Sustainable and Equitable Benefits?* Washington, D.C., September 7

Zelalem Temesgen 2009. Godare Forest and Possible Impacts of its Conversion to Oil Palm Plantation. In Ensermu et al (eds), pp. 133-151

- *Newspapers*

International

Arab News (Saudi Arabia) 18 August 2009

Bloomberg News Agency 10 November 2009

Financial Times 2009. Food crops harvested in Ethiopia come to Saudi Arabia, by Javier Blas. 6 March

Guardian 2010. Ethiopia- country of the silver sickle- offers land dirt cheap to farming giants, by Xan Rice. 15 February

New York Times 2009. Is There such a Thing as Agro-Imperialism?, by Andrew Rice.

22 November

Reuters 2009. Ethiopia sets aside land to foreign investors, by Tsegaye Tadesse. 29 July

Washington Post 2009. The ultimate crop rotation, by Stephanie McCrummen. 23 November

Local

Fortune (local business weekly): 2009 and 2010, various issues

Reporter (Amharic bi-weekly): 2009 and 2010, various issues

Government owned media

- *Video Film*

Gambella's Hidden Treasure, A VIP-HoAREC/N Production with EWCA, Produced by John Purdie, August 2010

- *Web sources*

GRAIN (International non-profit NGO based in Spain): www.grain.org 2009-2010

Ministry of Agriculture and Rural Development: www.moard.gov.et 2009-2010; since 2011, www.moa.gov.et and www.eap.gov.et

The Oakland Institute (US-based policy think tank): www.oaklandinstitute.org 2010

Friends of the Earth Europe: www.foeeurope.org

Persons Interviewed

Addis Ababa

- Araya Asfaw: Director, HoAREC, Addis Ababa University
- Van Aarst, Sanne: Coordinator, Parks and Buffer Zones Management Programme (HoAREC)
- Dereje Agonafer, Director, Environmental Units Program Directorate, EPA
- Diribu Jemal: Head, Bureau of Land and Environmental Protection, Oromia
- Milkessa Waqjirra: Acting Manager, Gambella Rice Project, Saudi Star Company
- Workafes Woldetsadik: Expert, Agricultural Investment Support Directorate, MOARD
- Yeneneh Teka: Director, Wildlife Development and Prevention Directorate, EWCA

Gambella

Key Informant Interviews in Terkodi Sub-Kebelle in Perpengo Kebelle

- Ouchan Oujuato; farmer
- Aryat Oujolu (female): farmer
- Tata Mao: farmer
- Agowa Okowa: farmer
- Oukelo Ouid: former Abobo woreda Administrator
- Oubong Oumed: Saudi Star employee
- [Name withheld]: Saudi Star employee

Focus Group discussion in Ouchok Ouchala sub-Kebelle, Tepi Kebelle

- Group of 12 men and 10 women
- [Name withheld]: farmer

Interviews in other places

- Ojul Ojul: Former Administrator of Annuak Zone (interviewed in Gambella town)
- Girma Wordin: Majangir public servant (interviewed while visiting Abobo town)
- [Name withheld]: Gumare Kebelle Presideent, Godere woreda, interviewed about Godere protest in Gambella town
- Gizachew Asre: Expert at Gambella Bureau of Agriculture (Gambella town)
- Aiymero Mekuria: Expert at Gambella Investment Commission (Gambella town)
- Informal discussion with Killil administration officials who requested anonymity

Bako Tibee Woreda

Key Informants Interviewed in Bechera Oda Gibe Kebelle

Farmers

- Gemechu Sobo
- Abrush Wodajo
- Shiferaw Wodajo
- Fekadu Benti
- Fekadu Wagjira
- Gudina Boru

Employees of Karuturi investment project

- Lellesa Tadesse: daily laborer
- Gete Bosho (female): daily laborer
- Getachew Oljirra : daily laborer
- Alemitu Berhanu (female): daily laborer
- Mohammed Ebbo: tractor operator

Focus Group Discussants (all farmers)

- Regassa Fuffa
- Tadesse Millet
- Oleqa Waqo
- Shibru Denussa
- Negasse Garumalle (female)
- Teffera Amente

Experts and Public Officials

- Banti Tolossa: Scientist and head of agricultural research center in Bako
- Gadissa Temesgen: Official at Woreda Investment Office

Other Interviews (towns people)

- Gemene Fetassa
- Fekadu Waggari
- Getachew Garri
- Zeynab Mohammed (female, tea vendor)

Annex 1

- *Notes on Information Update*

The research for this study was undertaken in October – December 2010 and the draft manuscript completed at the end of February 2011. Between then and the publication of the work there have been a number of developments which I was not able to incorporate in the text; these include the following : more investors have acquired land in various parts of the country; the rental fees recommended in the guidelines noted in the study are being used to determine rates by MOARD (which has now become MOA); copies of contracts signed between investors and MOARD have been posted on the latter's website; and the amount of land transferred to the federal land bank has increased as shown in the following table (cf with Table 1 in the text). *However, these developments in no way affect the arguments made in this paper and the conclusions arrived at.*

Table A1. Land Transferred to Federal Land Bank 2011

Killil	Land Transferred in Hectares
Benishangul	1,149,052
Gambella	1,226,893
Oromia	1,079,866
SNNP	180,604
Total	*3,636,415*

SOURCE: www.moard.gov.et "Investment Brusher" [sic] April 2011. The new portal of MOA is www.eap.gov.et

* ## *List of Investors Granted Land*

Table A2. Partial List of Large-Scale Land Transfers in Ethiopia (except Gambella)

Investor	Foreign Domestic	Land Size (Hectares)	Crops	Location
Al Habesh	Pakistan	28,000	Sugar estate	Wollega, Oro
Ambassel	Domestic	10,000	Biofuel crops	Metekel, BS
B&D Food	USA	18,000	Sugar estate	Awi, Amhara
Chadha Agro	India	122,000	Sugar, Biofuel	Oromia
Djibouti Gov't	Djibouti	3,000	Food crops	Bale, Oromia
Dubai World	Dubai	5,000	Tea	Illubabor, Oro
E. Africa Agric	Domestic	6,500	Food crops	Pawe, BeniShangul
Emami Biotech	India	80,000	Biofuel crops	Oromia
Finote Selaam	Domestic	5,000	Sesame	Guba, Benishangul
Flora EcoPower	German	13,000	Biofuel crops	E. Harage, Oro
Fri El Green	Italy	30,000	Biofuel crops	Omo Valley, SNNP
Global Energy	Israel	10,000	Biofuel	Wollaita, SNNP
IDC Invest	Danish	15,000	Biofuel	Assossa, BS
Kanan D Hills	India	10,000	Tea	SNNP
Karuturi	India	11,000	Rice, Biofuel	Bako, Oromia
P. Morrell	USA	10,000	Wheat	Bale, Oromia
N. Bank Egypt	Egypt	20,000	Food crops	Afar
Omo Sheleko	Domestic	5,500	Cotton, palm	SNNP
PetroPalm	German	50,000	Biofuel	Rayitu, Bale, Oro
SHAMPORJI	India	50,000	Biofuel	BeniShangul
Spentex	India	25,000	Cotton	Beni Shangul
Sun Biofuels	UK	5,000	Biofuel	Wollaita, SNNP
Sun Bio (NBC)	UK	80,000	Biofuel	Metekel, B.S
Sunrise Indust	India	15,000	Food	Oromia
Tomaisin	Israel	10,000	Food crops	Oromia
Vatic	India	20,000	Biofuel	Borena, Oromia
United Farm Bus	Domestic	3,000	Food crops	Bako, Oromia
Yehudi Hayun	Israel	10,000	Biofuel	Oromia

SOURCE: Findings from field visits, MOARD, MELCA Mahiber 2008, local press reports.
NOTE: Large-scale means 2000 hectares or more.

Table A3. Partial List of Large-Scale Land Transfers in Gambella

Investor	Foreign/ Domestic	Land Size (in Hectares)	Major Crops	Location
Alehilegn Worku	Domestic	2,000	Cotton, sesame	Abobo woreda
Bazel	Domestic	10,000	Cotton, sesame	Abobo woreda
BHO**	Indian	27,000	Rice, sesame	Itang woreda
Fiker PLC	Domestic	2,000	Cotton, sesame	Abobo woreda
Hussen Abera	Domestic	2,000	Sesame	Abobo woreda
Karuturi*	Indian	100,000	Rice, palm oil	Itang & Jikaw
Lucky Exports	Indian	5,000	Tea	Godere woreda
Muluken Azene	Domestic	2,000	Cotton, sesame	Abobo woreda
Ruchi Soya	Indian	25,000	Soya, palm oil	Goge woreda
Sannati Agro	Indian	10,000	Rice, pulses	Dimi woreda
Saudi Star**	Saudi Arabia	10,000	Rice, Soya	Abobo, Goge, Jore woredas
Solomon Kebede	Domestic	3,000	Cotton, sesame	Abobo woreda
Tewodros Abraham	Domestic	3,000	Sesame	Gambella Zuria
Yemane G/Mesk	Domestic	3,000	Sesame, maize	Gambella Zuria
Yetimgeta Mamo	Domestc	2,000	Sesame, maize	Itang woreda

SOURCE: Gambella Investment Commission, MOARD, local press reports

NOTE: Large-Scale here means 2000 hectares or more. Lease period: 50 years for all here except Ruchi which is   30 years.

*See Footnote 14 above

**According local press, Saudi Star applied for 129,000 hectares of additional land in Gambella and has been asked to prepare a business by the government (see above)

Total land transferred up to 2010 according to available records: 500,000 hectares.

Annex 2

- *Methodology*

We have used a wide variety of sources for this study, though gathering information for it proved to be unexpectedly difficult. There is an air of secrecy about the land deals, and the government has been economical with information. The spate of criticism of the investment program that appeared in the world media and in the web pages of international activist organizations may be partly to blame for this. We found it difficult to get interviews with senior officials of MOARD and EPA despite repeated attempts. Our effort to gather information in the Killils was relatively better but even here the information made available to us was not complete. While MOARD has established a website the information posted on it was dated and much of the material was of the promotional kind. The materials were later removed from the web pages.

I must also note the fact that the year 2010 was not a good year in Ethiopia to undertake studies which were dependent, as mine was, on cooperation from public agencies and officials. First there was the national election which took place in May, and then there was a series of nation-wide conferences by the ruling group of parties, both of which kept public officials busy and unavailable for consultation. The cabinet reshuffle that took place in September following the elections, and the mobilization of almost the entire civil service personnel in connection with the new and ambitious 5-year Growth and Transformation Plan did not make matters any easier.

Due to budget constraints we were able to undertake field visits and interviews in two sites only: in Gambella, which is over 700 kms away from Addis Ababa, and in Bako Tibee woreda in Oromia, 250 kms to the west of the capital. A short reconnaissance trip along the rift valley to Awassa in the SNNP helped us to identify important issues and to better frame questions for the field visits. In the end, we were able to interview key informants, eye witnesses, local towns people, undertake focus group discussions, hold meetings where possible with local, Killil and federal officials and gathered written information from government agencies in both sites as well as Addis Ababa. Two teams of data collectors were deployed in the field and additional staff was hired in the local areas. For Gambella, which takes two days to travel one way by road, I had to find a suitable person with knowledge of the area and the local language. This had a bearing in our choice of the site for the interviews. It is difficult to find a person who can speak all three major languages in Gambella, so when I finally found one he spoke the Anuak language only. Hence we had to choose Anuak Zone for our site. Within this, we selected Abobo woreda where Saudi Star, one of the largest foreign investors in the area, was located. In the case of Bako woreda, the language problem did not arise.

There was an unexpected hitch in Gambella which posed problems for our team there. The Killil's surprise resettlement (or villagization) program was launched just as the team arrived in the area, and for this and other reasons some interviewees asked for anonymity, and a few persons approached were reluctant to be interviewed. There was also a reshuffle of public officials and civil servants; the new officials did not have much knowledge of the investment program because they were not in office at the time the program was being implemented, so we had to search for those who knew about it but who were out of office now. The key informants included Annuak cultivators, a few Majangir individuals, Saudi Star workers, public officials, and town's people. Our focus group discussion involved some 22 persons, both male and female, in one village. We had asked only for eight to ten people but more came for the discussion because they were agitated by the resettlement program. In addition we were able to gather information from the Gambella's Investment Commission and the Bureau of Agriculture. We followed a more or less similar approach in Bako.

www.ingramcontent.com/pod-product-compliance
Lightning Source LLC
Chambersburg PA
CBHW080556270326
41929CB00019B/3328